Los Angeles

sunrise to sunset

Photography by
Dain Blair

Designed and Edited
by Sharon Poole Blair

December 6:40 am

Library of Congress Cataloging in Publication Data available.

ISBN: 978-0-9720618-03-5600

Printed in China.

immaginarepress.com

Immaginare Press
1418 2nd Street
Santa Monica, CA 90401
310.260.2626

December 6:59 am

Los Angeles, Sunrise to Sunset

A PHOTOGRAPHER'S PERSPECTIVE

For twenty years I have lived with my family in a most unique part of Los Angeles. At times I feel we are at the top of the world, when in fact we are simply two miles above Sunset Boulevard nestled in the hills of Brentwood.

The views are spectacular 365 days of the year. From our vantage point to the east are The J. Paul Getty Museum, downtown Los Angeles, East Los Angeles and the San Gabriel mountains.

Our direct view is southwest. We are just above West Los Angeles, looking out to Venice, Santa Monica, Marina Del Rey, Palos Verdes and Catalina Island. Views to the west are of Brentwood, Pacific Palisades, the Santa Monica mountains and the Channel Islands.

From sunrise to sunset, to the night lights that sparkle year long, I am never bored with the amazing views and the tranquility of living in the hills.

Inspired, I began to photograph and capture these remarkable moments from our property about ten years ago. On the pages that follow I share with you a perspective of the Los Angeles skies, from sunrise to sunset.

Dain Blair

January 7:08 am

October 7:31 am

May 6:42 am

December 5:45 – 5:51 pm

March 9:44am

July 6:23 am

November 7:08 – 7:11 pm

November 7:08 pm

December 4:43 pm

February 6:25 pm

January 5:27 – 5:32 pm

December 7:29 am

November 4:06 pm

November 8:53 am

November 8:55am

October 11:37 am

October 6:11 – 6:18 am

October 6:15am

December 11:43 am

October 11:53 am

August 6:28 pm Fire Cloud

December 5:18 – 5:34pm

November 5:47 pm

November 7:19 am

December 7:44 – 7:46 am

November 6:24 pm

March 9:07 am

September 6:43 – 6:49 pm

March 8:22 pm

September 6:45 pm

January 7:40 am

December 5:40 – 5:53 pm

November 7:09 am

October 6:03pm

November 5:49 pm

October 6:00 am

January 7:47 – 7:51 am

January 7:54 – 7:59 am

January 7:05 – 7:09 am

October 6:49 pm

October 6:36 am

October 8:17 pm

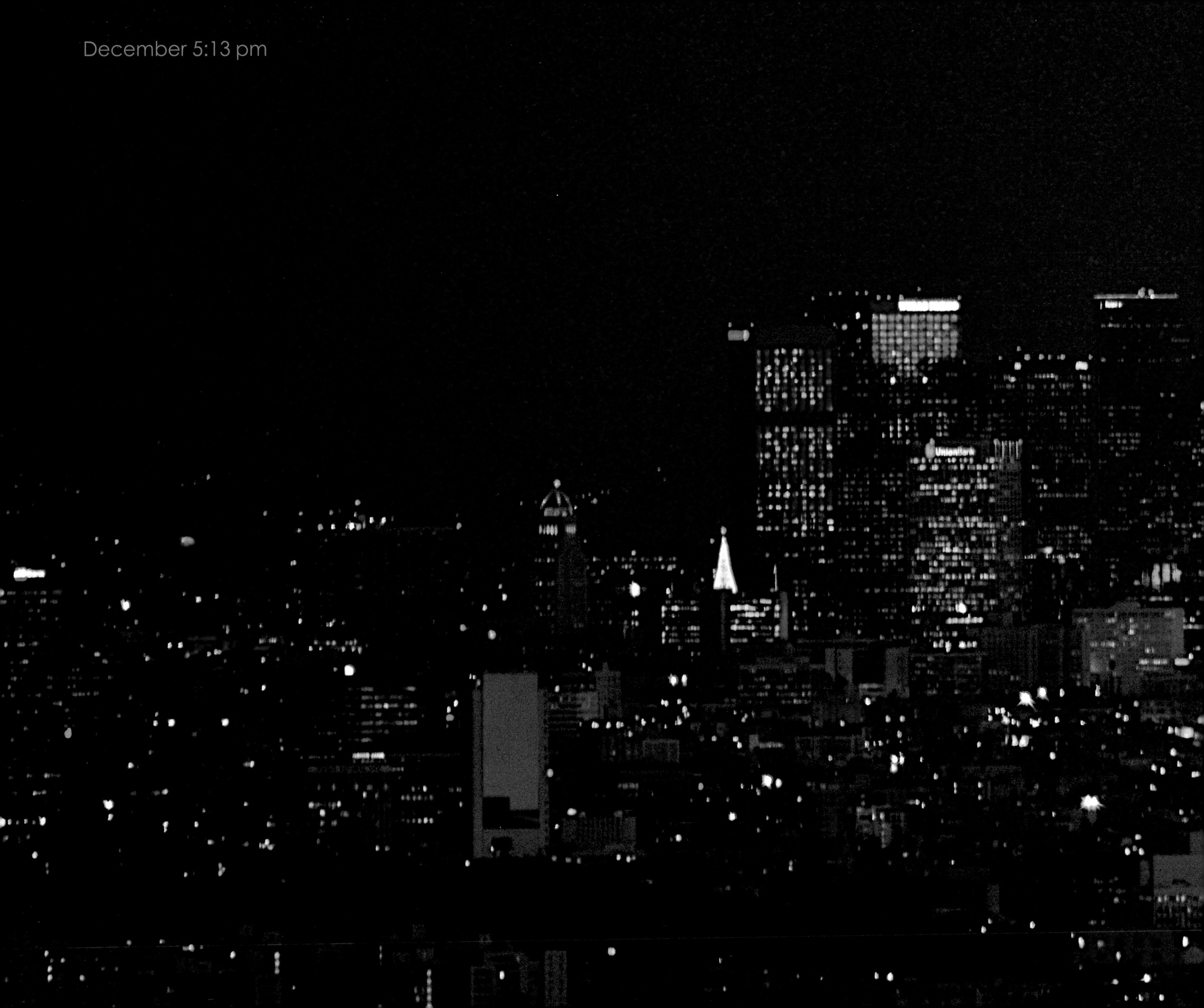

December 5:13 pm

October 8:18 pm

October 9:11 pm

November 6:12 am

September 6:36 pm

September 6:36 – 6:47 pm

August 8:02 pm

January 6:39 am

October 6:04 am

October 7:05 am

October 6:59 am

October 6:20 pm

October 6:49 pm

November 5:57 pm

November 11:54am

November 6:25 pm

November 12:01 pm

March 6:22am

October 12:44 pm

November 4:09 pm

January 7:54 – 7:59 am

January 7:59 am

October 7:55 am

October 7:04pm

October 7:44 am

October 6:37 am

October 5:03 – 5:21 pm

October 11:53pm

November 8:54 pm

October 7:22 pm

March 9:33 am

January 7:48 am

November 6:09 am

November 7:22 am

November 7:23 am

November 6:16 am

February 3:40 pm

January 6:23am

January 6:58 am

January 6:49 am

December 6:39 – 6:41 am

December 6:41 am

December 6:42 – 6:46 am

December 5:52 pm

November 8:09 am

December 4:52pm

Photographer - Dain Blair

Dain's experience covers everything from playing guitar and bass in touring bands, doing promotion for Capitol Records, producing artists with multiple chart records to the commercial music business. Dain started a custom music house, Groove Addicts, in 1996.

In addition to producing music for countless national TV spots, radio and TV imaging, his company scored TV shows like "Deal Or No Deal," "Extreme Makeover Home Edition," and "The Super Nanny," just to name a few. Dain has had the privilege of working with such talents as B.B. King, Jose Feliciano, Patti LaBelle, Danny Elfman, Stewart Copeland, Thomas Newman and numerous other feature film composers. Dain launched the Groove Addicts Production Music Catalog, which was sold to Warner Chappell Music in 2010 and the custom company was rebranded as Grooveworx and continues to do commercials, TV, radio imaging and music trailers.

After music, Dain's passion is photography. Over the past twenty years, Dain has taken thousands of photos using first his 35mm Nikon F1 and since the digital age his Nikon DSLR cameras with multiple lenses, but most notably his 17-35 wide angle. He enjoys photographing sunrises, sunsets and oceans and whenever possible both simultaneously. Dain spent a lot of time on the water growing up in the Panama Canal Zone, between the Pacific and Atlantic oceans. Each sunrise and sunset is unique and never to be repeated, so he is always looking for something that will be more impressive than the last one. He resides in Los Angeles with his wife, Sharon, and their two children, Justin and Taylor.